F. SCOT
FITZGERALD

A Life from Beginning to End

Copyright © 2022 by Hourly History.

Table of Contents

Introduction

Saint Paul, Minnesota, was a young city when Francis Scott Key Fitzgerald was born into it on September 24, 1896. The town had been founded just a few decades earlier when it was made into one of the great crossroads of train travel in the Midwestern United States.

Scott's father, Edward Fitzgerald, had moved to Minnesota from Maryland in 1890. It was here in Saint Paul that he met Molly, the future mother of F. Scott Fitzgerald, who was then more properly known by the name of Mary McQuillan. Molly's parents had arrived in America as virtual refugees from Ireland, fleeing the terrible conditions of famine that the Irish had been afflicted with in the 1840s, leading to what was tantamount to a mass exodus by the end of the decade.

Edward loved his wife, even though it's said a family member once remarked that she was "the most awkward and the homeliest woman I ever saw." Some may have seen Molly as socially awkward, but she was also quite bold. Truth be told, she was the outspoken member of the union since Edward was incredibly shy at the time. It's often been said that F. Scott Fitzgerald became an amalgamation of these two poles of personality he experienced with his parents.

Little Scott had a few older siblings, but all of them perished by 1900 due to various childhood illnesses. This meant that Scott was an only child until a little sister named Annabel arrived in 1901, and he would remain the only boy in the Fitzgerald home. Being the only son, he was both spoiled with affection from his doting mother and given high expectations by his hopeful father. As a result, Scott had a natural yet excruciating drive to succeed, and he didn't want to let anyone down.

Chapter One

Fateful Encounters of Youth

"My idea is always to reach my generation. The wise writer writes for the youth of his own generation, the critics of the next, and the schoolmasters of ever afterward."

—F. Scott Fitzgerald

The first big shock of F. Scott Fitzgerald's life was when his father was terminated from the position he held at Procter & Gamble. In many ways, the Fitzgerald family never really recovered from this blow. The job loss sent them back to Saint Paul, Minnesota (the family had moved to Buffalo specifically for Edward's job), and it relegated Mr. Fitzgerald to depend on his wife's inheritance money to survive. Edward and Molly would become more and more reclusive as a result, and a young F. Scott Fitzgerald—seeking to distance himself from his parents' perceived failure—would mention them less and less.

Scott began coursework at the prestigious St. Paul Academy in the fall of 1908, and here he studied the fine art of trying to pretend he was something he wasn't. The future writer tried to put on airs that he was just as much part of the upper crust as his high-rolling peers, even though his family was barely scraping by and his father had become a despondent drunk. He tried desperately to fit in with his peers through his participation with athletic organizations as well as intellectual clubs.

Scott's greatest success even in these early days was his writing. He worked on the school newspaper and even managed to craft an original—if not largely inspired by that other literary great Edgar Allan Poe—horror tale entitled *The Mystery of the Raymond Mortgage*. Yet despite his accomplishments in writing, Fitzgerald seemed to lag behind in other areas academically. It wasn't that he wasn't any less bright than his peers—he just didn't always apply himself as vigorously in one department as he would in another. As a consequence of this lack of effort, he was receiving poor marks in almost all of his classes.

It was due to the risk of him flunking out entirely that his parents decided to stage an intervention in 1911 by enrolling Scott in a private school called the Newman School, which was located in Hackensack, New Jersey. The going was rough, but Scott soon began to improve his academic standing. He also impressed his peers by becoming an excellent runner, winning accolades for the school's track team. The most important development by far was his mentorship by the resident priest, Father Sigourney Fay, who recognized Scott's budding talent as a writer and saw to it that he pursued that goal.

Fitzgerald graduated from the Newman School with the class of 1913 and then went on to Princeton University. The previous summer, Scott's grandmother had passed away. His family had already been living on inheritance money before that time, and through his grandmother's will, the family was infused with an additional $125,000 that she had left behind.

Before he enrolled at Princeton, Fitzgerald had briefly considered Harvard and Yale but changed his mind once he decided that Harvard was just a bit "too dull," and Yale was altogether "too crass" for his tastes. He was also impressed with Princeton's drama department since it featured the Triangle Club, a bastion of budding thespians who specialized in theatrical productions.

The lackadaisical Scott Fitzgerald had not properly prepped for the examination required to gain entrance to Princeton, however, and ended up bombing out. Fortunately for him, his talent was recognized despite his failings, and the gatekeepers at Princeton relaxed requirements just enough for Scott to squeeze through. Scott knew that since he had been given this special chance, he had to prove himself, and he was desperate to do so.

For this reason, he tried to join the football team, hoping that he could make up with athletics where he had previously faltered in academics. Scott was underweight though and proved unable to hold his own on the field, resulting in him getting rejected by the coordinators of the football team the first instance he got up enough courage to give it a try.

Once again, Fitzgerald would fall back on writing for his ultimate outlet. He began to work heavily, writing for theatrical productions for the Princeton Triangle Club, as well as doing work for the school publications such as the *Princeton Tiger*, which produced comedic and light-hearted articles. He also joined a so-called eating club at Princeton called the University Cottage Club. The concept of an eating club may seem odd to modern readers, but these were essentially a kind of fraternity in which members would meet in dining halls to share a meal as well as intellectual thoughts and pursuits amongst each other.

The gathering that would have the most impact among F. Scott Fitzgerald would not be at an eating club but rather a Christmas festival back at Saint Paul where he met a charming girl by the name of Ginevra King. Although in Scott's personal romantic life, Ginevra would forever be the one that got away, she would go on to inspire a whole stream of literary characters in his greatest works of fiction.

Chapter Two

Serving in World War I

"When people are taken out of their depths they lose their heads, no matter how charming a bluff they may put up."

—F. Scott Fitzgerald

Scott Fitzgerald met the attractive young socialite Ginevra King in Saint Paul in early 1915 while on Christmas break from Princeton. She hailed from a wealthy family who lived in a prestigious suburb of Chicago called Lake Forest. Her parents had shipped her off from Chicagoland to Minnesota so that she could attend a prestigious boarding school for girls called Westover School. Here, she had befriended a girl that Scott knew growing up—Midge Hersey.

During breaks, rather than going back to Illinois, Ginevra would often spend her holiday with Midge's family in Saint Paul. It was Midge that brought Ginevra to the Christmas celebration in Saint Paul, where Ginevra met the then 19-year-old F. Scott Fitzgerald. Scott and Ginevra would see each other off and on over the next couple of years.

Fitzgerald was deeply fixated on Ginevra, although for Ginevra, Scott was really just one more in a line of steady suitors. Starting in 1916, it seems that she began to slowly distance herself from Scott, with their meetings becoming fewer and farther between. Toward the end of their relationship, most of their dealings would be from afar through the letters they would write each other.

In these letters—some of which have been preserved to this very day—Scott's love for Ginevra is captured for posterity. In one letter, Scott passionately wrote her, "Oh, it's hard to write you what I really feel when I think of you so much. You've gotten to mean to me a dream that I can't put on paper anymore."

Ginevra must have been equal parts flattered and alarmed to hear Scott pour out his heart like this. She had come to a crossroads and needed to now either continue to encourage the infatuated writer or to slowly disentangle herself from him altogether. Since her rich parents naturally frowned upon Scott's meager upbringing, she would ultimately choose the latter and continue the long slow drift away from F. Scott Fitzgerald.

Even so, the letters would continue, and Scott would continue to hold out hope of recapturing the early days of their romance. In 1917, Ginevra finally let Scott know she was going to have to end the relationship. As one could imagine, Fitzgerald was heartbroken; some say he was even on the brink of suicide.

It was in the terrible aftermath of this breakup that Scott decided to join the army, just as the U.S. was being drawn into World War I. Life stateside now seemed unbearable, so F. Scott Fitzgerald decided to try his luck in the trenches instead. His grades had been failing him for quite some time at this point as well, and whether or not he would ever graduate from Princeton was long in doubt. As such, when he dropped out of Princeton in October of 1917, joining the army when a major global conflagration was afoot probably seemed like the best exit strategy available to Scott at the time.

Despite his intentions, Scott would not end up on the battlefields of Europe after all. He arrived at Fort Leavenworth in November and was put under the charge of a later much more famous commander named Dwight D. Eisenhower. After a few months at Leavenworth, Scott was shipped off to Camp Zachary Taylor in Louisville, Kentucky, for a brief pitstop before going on to Camp Gordon in Augusta, Georgia. He was then sent off to Camp Sheridan in Montgomery, Alabama.

Although he managed to rise up to the officer class of second lieutenant, Fitzgerald found himself unable to give or take orders very well. He didn't have much sympathy for the men under his charge, and on one occasion, when they expressed disdain for the food they had to eat at camp, his answer to their complaint was simply to force them to march. Instead of finding solutions to their problems, he would punish them for complaining. On another occasion, Scott almost created a friendly fire incident when he accidentally ordered troops to fire a mortar with live rounds at another group of soldiers.

It could be speculated that part of Scott's reasoning for joining the military was a last-ditch attempt to impress Ginevra. After a painful breakup with the woman they love, many young men will go to extreme lengths to try to rekindle their interest. Perhaps Fitzgerald thought that if he donned a dashing uniform and became a celebrated military officer, his heroics could regain him his lost love.

As is so often the case in such situations, while he was out on the rebound trying to reinvent himself, Scott met another girl that would, for a time, take his mind off of Ginevra. A native of Montgomery Alabama, her name was Zelda Sayre. Zelda came from a prominent southern family with deep roots in southern culture and politics. Her father, in fact, sat on Alabama's State Supreme Court.

Despite the stalwart and respected members of her family tree, Zelda was rambunctious and unpredictable from the beginning. She was known to go against the norms and wasn't afraid to stand out in the crowd if she wanted to get a point across. It was perhaps this boldness, which to some came off as a bit eccentric, that attracted Scott. Although he had distanced himself from his mother's own unusually bold behavior, he found himself drawn to that very same quality in this young woman.

Scott met Zelda for the first time in the summer of 1918 when the two attended a local country club dance. They were both rather taken with each other and were soon a regular item. Just like Ginevra's well-to-do family, Zelda's family was not too thrilled about Scott, but the headstrong Zelda was more than willing to go against her father's wishes and continued to see Scott regardless.

Their courtship was only put on hold on October 26, 1918, when Scott and his fellow contingent of troops were scheduled to head overseas to join their fellow troops on the Western Front. As fate would have it though, there would be no need since an armistice ending the war ended up being signed by the warring parties on November 11, 1918.

You would think that F. Scott Fitzgerald might be happy at these results—so many of his peers had, after all, died in the trenches—but he was not. Scott felt that he had missed a great opportunity to prove himself in battle, and without it, he had lost yet another chance to make himself a man of great social distinction. The young man felt that his opportunity for greatness had once again eluded him.

Chapter Three

Fitzgerald's First Novel

"All good writing is swimming under water and holding your breath."

—F. Scott Fitzgerald

Just prior to leaving the army, F. Scott Fitzgerald had composed his very first, full-length novel, a piece he called *The Romantic Egotist*. The novel heavily revolved around his time at Princeton and, even more importantly, his time with Ginevra. He sent a draft of the novel to the book publisher Scribner's, but it was ultimately declined publication.

Even though this early draft was passed up, the man who looked it over—Max Perkins—was impressed enough to reach out to Scott and ask him to revise the novel. Perkins insisted that he polish it up a bit and resubmit an improved draft later on. For some budding writers, such remarks might seem to amount merely to professional pity and an effort to let the author of a bad bill of goods down easy. In this case though, it seems that Perkins truly was giving his honest opinion; as we will see, it was once Fitzgerald revised and refurbished this basic framework that he would finally break out as a rising star in the literary world.

Fitzgerald was meanwhile discharged from his military duties in the spring of 1919. Unknown to others, he had secretly carried the macabre dream of having his novel published just before dying on the battlefields of Europe. When the armistice came, this grandiose vision obviously would not be coming to fruition. Instead, Scott and Zelda became engaged.

Upon his discharge, Scott temporarily put his relationship with Zelda on hold and made his way to New York. Here, he holed himself up in a tiny Manhattan apartment and began working in advertising for the Barron Collier advertising agency. During the day, he wrote up catchy jingles for various advertisements, and at night, he feverishly produced short stories and screenplays. All of these efforts would be rejected, with the sole exception of a short story called "Babes in the Woods," which was published in a New York magazine called *TheSmart Set*. Even this success was a bit discouraging since the story itself was one that he had written years before at Princeton. All of his newer material was steadily being rejected.

Matters would get even worse for Scott when he visited Zelda in Montgomery that summer, only for her to break off their engagement, informing him that he just wasn't financially stable enough for marriage. Completely distressed at what his life had become, an entirely disillusioned and dejected F. Scott Fitzgerald decided to quit his job at the advertising agency in New York.

Fitzgerald then went back to his hometown of Saint Paul to stay with his parents. One can only imagine just how defeated this ambitious young man must have felt. Very near suicidal, his only solace was alcohol, as he tried to deaden the pain and disappointment that had become the ever-present reminders of his own perceived failings.

Yet somewhere in the midst of all of this mental anguish, Fitzgerald found the will to struggle on. Pulling out his old manuscript for the story he had previously called *The Romantic Egotist*, he began to make rapid revisions of the draft, which would lead to the rendering of his first smash hit, ultimately re-titled *This Side of Paradise*. Drawn largely from personal experience, the novel became a classic coming-of-age story of a young man struggling to find his way in life. Since it was taken directly from Scott's own struggles, the novel immediately resonated as a timely and realistic presentation.

This time around when Scott sent the novel off to the publishing house, he almost immediately got a bite. He sent the work back to Scribner's on September 3, and it was approved for publication by September 16. Although nothing was guaranteed at this point, the very fact that his book was accepted by the publisher instilled the then 23-year-old F. Scott Fitzgerald with great confidence—so much so that he immediately went back to New York to once again embark upon the life of a full-time novelist.

Chapter Four

Marriage and Children

*"I don't suppose I really know you very well—but
I know you smell like the delicious grass that
grows near old walls and that your hands are
beautiful opening out of your sleeves and that the
back of your head is a mossy sheltered cave when
there is trouble in the wind and that my cheek just
fits the depression in your shoulder."*

—Zelda Fitzgerald

Scott Fitzgerald arrived back on the New York
scene in late 1919; it was just prior to the Roaring
Twenties of which the stylings of his work would
be forever associated. It was that same year that
prohibition was enacted in an attempt to end
alcoholic consumption in the United States. This
would lead to bootlegged alcohol and illegal
gatherings called speakeasies, where the now
illegal beverages would be served.

The illicit and rebellious nature of social life in America seemed to fit right in with the themes of Fitzgerald's literature. Despite the prohibition, as soon as he was making big bucks from his published works, Scott was known to be a regular fixture on the speakeasy scene, lavishly spending money on his and his friends' alcoholic consumption.

By the New Year of 1920, however, the writer had found himself understandably burnt out. In a bid to rid himself of some of his excesses and to find a place where he could once again sit down and write, he decided to momentarily leave the high life of New York behind in exchange for a quiet retreat in New Orleans, Louisiana. He also hoped that a return to the south would aid him in his quest of re-starting his relationship with Zelda, who was still in Montgomery, Alabama, at the time. Scott was successful in this pursuit. After paying a visit to her parents' home in Montgomery, Zelda informed her folks that the engagement was back on track.

Although relieved that Fitzgerald seemed to have achieved financial stability, her parents harbored some concern over his Catholic background. The Sayres were staunch Episcopalian Protestants, but as long as Scott was able to provide a stable home life for their daughter, they were willing to look past it. It was perhaps Zelda's mother, Minnie, who put it best when she declared, "A good Catholic is as good as any other man and that is good enough. It will take more than the Pope to make Zelda good; you will have to call on God Almighty direct."

With his patched-up relationship with Zelda in the works, Fitzgerald returned to New York in February of 1920, where he set up shop and waited for Zelda to come join him. This time though, it was Zelda who began to have misgivings. Initially, she wasn't too thrilled about leaving her old lifestyle behind for the glitz and glamor of New York City. Despite the bravado she displayed in front of her parents, she also still had some doubts about Scott's long-term success. Nevertheless, she did indeed arrive in New York as planned, and Scott and Zelda were wed right there in the Big Apple at St. Patrick's Cathedral on April 3, 1920.

After exchanging their vows, the couple made sure that their honeymoon was an extravagant affair in luxury suites at the Commodore and Biltmore Hotels. Their behavior was rowdy to the extreme at both, and the couple was actually kicked out of the Biltmore when the hotel manager had had enough. Several other guests had apparently complained about Scott and Zelda's behavior, and the fed-up manager finally listened to their gripes by removing the source of the problem—Scott and Zelda.

Even then, the couple were not to be outdone and famously spent the better part of a half-hour going through the hotel's revolving door. One can only imagine the drunken yet completely childish display that the pair put on for the infuriated hotel management.

Besides wreaking havoc at hotels, the newlyweds also caused many a scene by visiting theatrical productions and deliberately laughing at inappropriate times. It was certainly good fun for them but probably wasn't too well received by the struggling actors on stage or the writers who had written the scripts. At this point, Fitzgerald didn't really care; he was riding high on life, and he could care less about what others thought. It was precisely this carelessness that often had him rubbing others the wrong way ever since his days at Princeton.

At any rate, the following summer, Scott and Zelda finally decided to settle down a bit. They moved into a more permanent residence by way of a beach house located in Westport,

Connecticut, but rather than simply leaving the party, they ended up bringing the party to them. This beachfront mansion—with all of its wild, drunken get-togethers—would in many ways help shape the backdrop of Scott's later novel, *The Great Gatsby*.

All the wild partying would hit a much-needed speed bump when Zelda found out that she was pregnant in the spring of 1921. As raucous as Zelda had become, even she knew that the introduction of this new little life meant that they would have to slow down. Still, they decided to have one last great hurrah together before Zelda would be too heavily pregnant to do so.

The couple booked a trip to England and set sail by way of an ocean liner called the *Aquitania* that May. Upon their arrival, they visited all of the usual museums and attractions before making their way across the English Channel to France. This then kicked off a whirlwind tour of Europe that would take them all the way to Rome.

Come July, Scott and Zelda finally decided to return and made their way back stateside. The couple then ended up renting out a house on the outskirts of Saint Paul, Minnesota, as they awaited the arrival of their first child. This child would arrive on October 26, and in a nod to her father, the baby girl was named Frances Scott Fitzgerald but would be subsequently called "Scottie" for short. With barely time to take a breath, life was moving faster and faster for the Fitzgeralds, accelerating by the minute.

Chapter Five

A Lavish Lifestyle

"Though the Jazz Age continued, it became less and less an affair of youth. The sequel was like a children's party taken over by the elders."

—F. Scott Fitzgerald

After becoming parents, Scott and Zelda would often feel more burdened by the responsibilities therein than they were exhilarated at the results. Although they certainly loved their child, the young couple was just not yet ready for parenthood. Still, they tried their best and momentarily left New York behind for the much more sedate trappings of Saint Paul, Minnesota.

Along with caring for his newfound offspring, Fitzgerald embarked upon his next novel called *The Beautiful and Damned.* The book depicted the married life of two characters named Anthony and Gloria Patch, who mirrored the habits of him and his own wife, Zelda. The book was well-received, and about 40,000 copies were purchased in the first year alone.

Fitzgerald then entered into a deal to sell the film rights to *The Beautiful and Damned* as well as *This Side of Paradise*, netting himself an additional $12,500. These successes were followed by further profits gleaned from the publication of *Tales of the Jazz Age*, an anthology of Scott's short stories, which hit the shelves in the fall of 1922. Fitzgerald was doing well, and it seemed that he had embarked upon a successful cycle of living it up with his wife Zelda, having his art imitate his life in books so that he could make more money, and then proceeding to live it up even further.

It was riding on this wave of success and an influx of cold, hard cash that Scott and Zelda made their way back to New York in 1922. This time around, they took up residence in a home in Long Island, near the city of Great Neck. This provided them with a stable home life, yet it was still close enough to the action so that a trip on over to New York City proper would never be out of the question.

Around this time, Fitzgerald produced a series of short stories that he would later identify as being "second-rate" just to keep a steady flow of income coming. His primary effort would meanwhile be the work of transforming a previous short story called "The Vegetable or From President to Postman" into a play. Ever since his Princeton days, Scott had dreamed of being a successful playwright, and he took advantage of his close proximity to Broadway and his growing connections in the literary world to make that happen.

The Vegetable would be a departure from his usual formula, and instead of madcap romantic drama, it featured full-on political satire. The story centered around a drunken railroad clerk who sobers up to find that he's somehow running for president of the United States. Taking license from Fitzgerald's own history of drunken binges, the story uses the absurd trappings of a hopeless drunk turned presidential candidate as a vehicle for ironic humor and political/social commentary.

It wasn't a bad plot device, but the long-winded remarks and sequences that Fitzgerald crafted proved a bit too much for audience-goers to follow. After the play premiered on November 10, 1923, Fitzgerald was horrified to find that the audience was so bored out of their minds that many theatergoers decided to get up out of their seats and leave. Not willing to see the entire play through, many forfeited the money spent on admission just to get away from the debacle they saw being played out. The reception was so negative, in fact, that the production was shut down in a matter of days.

Fitzgerald's finances were already in the red due to he and his wife's extravagant spending, and now that any potential profits from *The Vegetable* had been lost, Scott found himself in desperate need to recoup. As such, he momentarily swore off partying and alcohol and hunkered down in Great Neck. Here, he worked around the clock to hammer out several short stories. These he then sold to various publications just so he could pay off the looming debt that he had accrued.

He hoped that from here on out, he would be on easy street, but F. Scott Fitzgerald was finding that he was just a few miscalculations away from being more broke than he had ever been before.

Chapter Six

The Great Gatsby

*"I wish now I'd never relaxed or looked back—
but said at the end of The Great Gatsby: I've
found my line—from now on this comes first. This
is my immediate duty—without this I am
nothing."*

—F. Scott Fitzgerald

Looking to make a new start, in May of 1924, Scott, Zelda, and their little baby girl packed their things and headed over to Paris, France. Fitzgerald wanted to make a clean break with his riotous living in New York, and he felt that a brand-new city, where he knew next to no one, just might do the trick.

Paris had become a mecca for ex-pat American artists, so although he was technically a stranger in the city, it wouldn't be long before Scott found his niche. The first real friends that the Fitzgeralds made upon their arrival in Paris were the American transplants Gerald and Sara

Murphy. Gerald was a Yale man who had made his way to France with his wife Sara shortly after graduating. He was a budding artist who studied among the Cubists.

Despite this newfound social support, Scott and Zelda's marriage would run into some serious trouble when Zelda began an affair with a Frenchman whom she met at a nearby French naval base. Zelda was in many ways recreating her youth since in her Montgomery days when she had first met Scott—who himself was a dashing young military officer at the time— flirting with local soldiers and sailors was all part of her normal routine.

Her flirtation turned into an all-out fling, however, and it would prove to be a critical turning point in her marriage to Scott. The soldier was soon transferred, and Scott didn't even know that the illicit liaisons had occurred. As it turns out, Zelda was so guilt-ridden afterward that she confessed the whole thing in full. Fitzgerald decided to forgive his wife and try his best to move on, but their relationship would never be the same again. Zelda, in particular, began to have mental breakdowns and even seemed to be suicidal. On at least one occasion, she appears to have attempted to take her life when she took an inordinate amount of sleeping pills before going to bed.

Along with all of this, both Scott and Zelda returned heavily to the booze. In a drunken haze, the pair—with child in tow—made their way to Rome after their lease was up at their home in Paris. The stay in Rome would be brief, however, since in January of 1925, Scott would make the mistake of assaulting an Italian police officer while in a drunken rage. The whole incident began when Fitzgerald got into an altercation with a local cab driver. Scott didn't agree with how much the cabbie was charging him, and a shouting match ensued. It was then that an off-duty Italian police officer attempted to diffuse the situation. Scott wasn't going to have it, however, and proceeded to punch the man out.

Even though the off-duty officer was apparently down for the count, the act did not go unnoticed, and soon more police officers converged on the scene and hauled the writer right off to jail. Zelda then had to figure out a way to come up with bail money, even as her husband was being tormented by a gang of vengeful Italian policemen in a prison cell. As soon as Zelda sprang Scott lose, the Fitzgeralds fled Rome for the Island of Capri, a quiet refuge in the Bay of Naples.

Throughout all of this turmoil, Fitzgerald had been intermittently working on what would become his masterpiece, *The Great Gatsby*. It was while he and his wife were recuperating in Rome that he drafted his last revision of the epic and fired it off to his publisher in the spring of 1925.

The true genius of *The Great Gatsby* was its use of the character Nick Carraway as a narrator of the main events, yet who acts as almost an innocent bystander, describing the extravagance of the main characters. Nick, a humble Midwesterner, is presented as an outsider to all the drama and, in that sense, seems to share the reader's bewilderment with the insanity of Gatsby and the other main characters as the narrative progresses.

The greatest conflict of the story is that the extravagant Gatsby is a self-made rich man, yet he is relentlessly pursuing the love of his life, Daisy Buchanan (another character modeled after Ginevra), who is from old money. Gatsby learns that no matter how much money he makes, it doesn't immediately buy him into the social world of those born into several generations of inherited wealth.

Scott Fitzgerald, no doubt, felt the same way about himself. Even though he was a successful writer and was making a lot of money, in the eyes of the wealthiest American socialites, their old money world would always trump the aspirations of this self-made up-start. No matter what he did, Fitzgerald would never be considered one of them.

Although *The Great Gatsby* would become known as F. Scott Fitzgerald's masterwork, he would not get to enjoy such accolades during his lifetime. It would take decades for the book to catch on with a wider audience, and to Scott and his publisher's chagrin, the book would barely sell 20,000 copies by the end of the year. During his lifetime, *TheGreat Gatsby* would remain a marketing failure. Although critics loved the book, the general public just didn't seem to take much of an interest. It was only after Fitzgerald's passing that the book would develop a cult following, leading to a triumphant revival. Back in the 1920s, the fruits of these labors remained elusive.

Chapter Seven

Mental Breakdown

"Family quarrels are bitter things. They don't go according to any rules. They're not like aches or wounds; they're more like splits in the skin that won't heal because there's not enough material."

—F. Scott Fitzgerald

In the aftermath of the marketing failures for *The Great Gatsby*, Scott's only saving grace was the fact that the story was optioned for both a theatrical production and a Hollywood film, which led to additional profits for Scott, amounting to around $35,000. This was certainly a good chunk of cash at the time, but the fact that the book sales were so dismal remained incredibly frustrating for Fitzgerald, who was convinced that he had just wrapped up an American masterpiece.

Disappointed, he was back in France by the New Year of 1926, hammering away at what would be his next novel. During this time,

Fitzgerald became acquainted with many ex-pat writers; most notably, he grew close to a young Ernest Hemingway whom he had initially encountered sometime in the summer of 1925. Hemingway was a World War I veteran who—unlike Scott—had seen action during the war and walked away a highly decorated soldier.

After coming back stateside, Hemingway got a job as a reporter before heading off to Paris to work as a foreign correspondent. By 1926, Hemingway, who had previously been little known, had his work making the rounds in a collection of short stories called *In Our Time*. It wasn't long before Hemingway was being bandied about as the next great American novelist. In other words, he was viewed as a successor to F. Scott Fitzgerald himself.

Despite the opportunity for rivalry, Fitzgerald professed his admiration for Hemingway's work, and the two became good friends. Nevertheless, it is said that Hemingway occasionally expressed contempt for Fitzgerald's drinking habits and most especially his relationship with Zelda. Hemingway seemed to think that Zelda was a bad influence on Scott and that she was even stifling his writing. Hemingway would later claim that he even witnessed Zelda actively trying to sabotage her husband's work in fits of jealousy. As he put it, she "encouraged her husband to drink so as to distract Fitzgerald from his work on his novel."

Zelda didn't like Hemingway too much either and became fond of calling Ernest "bogus," claiming that his "rugged persona" was just a schtick. She also occasionally accused Scott and Ernest of being lovers. Whatever the case may be, Fitzgerald was not very productive between the spring of 1926 and the summer of 1927 as he and Zelda appeared to lurch from one alcohol-fueled evening to the next without much to show for it.

Still, Fitzgerald's publisher Scribner's was able to capitalize on previous short stories. A collection of Scott's works called *All the Sad Young Men* came out in February of 1926 with moderate success. The influx of money from this publication would at least keep the Fitzgeralds afloat for a while.

Scott, Zelda, and their daughter then returned to the United States in December, ready to start a new chapter in their lives. That chapter seemed to arrive in January of 1927 when Fitzgerald was offered work in Hollywood for a production company called United Artists. The company wanted Scott to recreate the magic of his previous work on the big screen. They were willing to give him a $3,500 advance and another $12,500 once his screenplay was complete.

Leaving their child with Scott's parents, the couple went off to California, where they booked a room in the famed Ambassador Hotel in Los Angeles. It wasn't long before they were hobnobbing with the stars of the day, such as Mary Pickford, Douglas Fairbanks, and John Barrymore. Here, however, they found that their previous carefree lifestyle and routine hijinks did not go over as well on the Hollywood social scene. More often than not, rather than endear anyone with them, the couple's eccentricities just made them come off as incredibly odd. This was certainly the case when they went to a costume ball held by movie mogul Samuel Goldwyn and proceeded to crawl on all fours and bark like dogs. Rather than getting a good drunken laugh like they were used to, they were given derisive stares.

Even worse than this, Fitzgerald's screenplay was rejected, and he never received the promised $12,500. Disappointed, Scott and his wife headed back to the East Coast, where they set up shop in a house in Delaware. Sliding back into despondency and numbed by alcohol, most of their evenings turned into prolonged drinking fests, in which they would invite their friends to take part in their mischief. The more they drank, the worse Zelda and Scott's disagreements became, and soon they were even getting violent with each other. This domestic violence would lead to Fitzgerald getting on the wrong side of the law on multiple occasions.

Due to all of these disruptions, he was having a decidedly hard time finishing up his latest novel, and so seeking a change, he decided to move his family to Paris, France, once again. Matters would soon get drastically out of hand when, in 1930, during a car ride in Paris, Zelda grabbed the steering wheel and attempted to send the car off the road. This incident could not be so easily forgotten, and in the aftermath, Zelda was taken in for psychiatric evaluation. During this evaluation, she was given the diagnosis of schizophrenia. Scott would try his best to comfort his wife in her condition, but now it seemed that absolutely nothing could keep their stormy marriage together.

Chapter Eight

The Crack-Up

"In a real dark night of the soul, it is always three o'clock in the morning, day after day."

—F. Scott Fitzgerald

Scott Fitzgerald's latest sojourn in France was interrupted when he received news in early 1931 that his father Edward had passed away. The death was sudden and abrupt, and Scott was shocked to learn of it. Although he had distanced himself from his father in the past, he still loved the man. As such, he dropped everything, hopped on an ocean liner, and sailed back to the States.

Fitzgerald attended the funeral, and in his own personal notes at the time, he fondly recalled, "I loved my father—always deep in my subconscious I have referred judgment back to him, what he would have thought or done. He loved me—and felt a deep responsibility for me." As much as Scott had tried to distance himself from his parents whom he viewed as social failures, he still loved them deep down, and this instance makes that clear.

During his time in the United States, he also stopped by Zelda's family in Montgomery, Alabama. He had since come to find out that her family had a history of mental illness. Despite this being the case, many of her relatives pointed fingers at Fitzgerald, feeling that the wild lifestyle he encouraged was a major factor in Zelda's breakdown.

Zelda, for her part, seemed to come around while Scott was gone and even missed her husband. They say that absence makes the heart grow fonder, and this was the first time in a long time that the two seemed to express genuine love for one another. In one letter, Zelda wrote her husband, "You are so infinitely sweet and dear— Oh my dear—my love, my infinitely inexpressible sweet darling dear, I love you so much."

By the time Scott made his way back to Europe, Zelda seemed to be on the mend, and she was released from psychiatric care on September 15, 1931. Upon his wife's release, Fitzgerald took the family back to the U.S. Here, he rented a home in Cloverdale, Alabama, figuring that Zelda would be able to recover best near her family in Montgomery.

Due to Zelda's medical care, Fitzgerald had new bills to pay, and as such, he found himself once again working around the clock to pump out short stories that he could sell for various publications. Needless to say, it wasn't enough, and by the fall of 1931, Scott was once again looking for a more immediate means to supplement his income. Thus, when Fitzgerald was once again courted by Hollywood in November of 1931, he leaped at the opportunity. It was the esteemed Hollywood producer Irving Thalberg who wanted Scott to craft a script for a comedic piece entitled *Red-Headed Woman*. For this work, Thalberg was willing to pay Scott $1,200 a week.

The promise of a steady paycheck certainly trumped the meager lump sum amounts that Fitzgerald was getting to pump out short stories, so without hesitation, Scott accepted the offer and made his way to Hollywood. He would continue his bad track record with screenplays, however, and by the end of the year, he was already terminated from the project. He was sent packing with just $6,000 to show for his troubles.

Despite the embarrassment, the influx of money was indeed helpful enough for Fitzgerald's ever so troubled financial situation. Over the next few years, he hunkered down and finally managed to finish his next full-length novel, a piece he called *Tender is the Night*. The book hit store stands in the spring of 1934, with both positive and negative reviews. Some critics enjoyed the material well enough, but others voiced their misgivings, stating that the overall effort was rather sub-par when compared to everything else that Fitzgerald had done in the past.

Even worse for the cash-strapped Fitzgerald was that once again, he found his latest novel unable to garner much interest among the general public. Selling only around 12,000 copies at its outset, it was yet another failed enterprise. Fitzgerald, who had penned his greatest work during the 1920s, was now coming to consider the fact that the times had changed. The world was rocked by a stock market crash in 1929, and the early 1930s were in the throes of a global financial depression. The jazz had worn way too thin for his work to gain suitable interest. Rather than a vanguard of the new generation, F. Scott Fitzgerald was fast becoming a relic of the past.

In the aftermath of poor book sales following the release of his latest full-length novel, Fitzgerald was emotionally shattered. Adding to his misery, his wife was frequently in and out of psych wards, and his own health was facing a precipitous decline due to his many years of alcoholism. As depressed and despondent as he was though, he knew that he had to struggle on. He began to hammer out a series of short stories that he hoped to sell to magazines to at least provide a meager income to support himself and his family. Unfortunately, the anthology entitled *Taps at Reveille* was not received well, and even this effort fell flat on its face.

During this period, despite doctors' warnings, Fitzgerald continued to drink, and in his loneliness and desperation, he also took on mistresses. While his wife was away at psychiatric clinics, he began to see various other women. Yet even though he was now thoroughly unfaithful, he couldn't bring himself to completely abandon his wife and continued to foot the bill for her extensive treatments, with what little money he still had in his dwindling savings.

As the situation became dire, Fitzgerald staged his own intervention in 1935 by abruptly cutting off all of his friends and traveling to the remote reaches of Hendersonville, North Carolina, to hole up in a hotel, sober up, and face his demons head-on. He would later refer to the period as his "crack-up" or "nervous breakdown," in which he had to allow himself to fall flat on his face in order to pick himself up again.

Like many alcoholics, Fitzgerald had spent years trying to mask his problems and was desperately on the defensive to prevent anyone from knowing the full scope of his situation. Here, in Hendersonville, he finally allowed himself to completely collapse so that he could begin picking himself up from the rubble that his life had become.

During this moment of powerful reflection, Fitzgerald penned three autobiographical works which he would refer to as his "crack-up essays." In them, he analyzed his troubles and came to the conclusion that he suffered from "a moral drift" in which he believed that he had fallen so far from his glory days of the past that he would never be as good a man again. He then rationalized that he had simply been trying to be someone he was not in the first place. Fitzgerald was now determined not to try too hard to impress others but to simply be himself. As he put it, "The man I had persistently tried to be became such a burden that I have cut him loose."

Fitzgerald re-emerged from this session of self-discovery a new man, and instead of dreading what the public might think of him, as the New Year of 1936 dawned, he sold these intimate essays to Esquire, unashamed of what his life story had become. Sadly enough, the effort backfired in the most terrible way when other writers—including his old friend Ernest Hemingway—began to deride Scott's intimate confessions.

Even worse, in September of 1936, the *New York Post* published what amounted to a mockumentary about Fitzgerald called "The Other Side of Paradise," in which he was further ridiculed for his drunkenness and other perceived foibles, heavily drawing its inspiration from Scott's own crack-up essays.

In considering Fitzgerald's downfall in the press, his treatment seems to mirror that of many celebrities throughout the decades. It's often been cited that the press and the public in general love to build up celebrities and then publicly tear them down. It seems that F. Scott Fitzgerald, who was an icon of the Roaring Twenties, was finding himself thoroughly loathed and despised by the

1930s. Fitzgerald thought that he would gain sympathy by opening his heart to the world with his intimate essays, but he only added fuel to the fire of his own demise.

Chapter Nine

Late Life and Death

"There are no second acts in American lives."

—F. Scott Fitzgerald

With the complete collapse of his public persona and the complete failure of his work to gain traction, Fitzgerald found himself heavily in debt. In order to pay for his wife's medical bills as well as the cost to put his now teenaged daughter Scottie through boarding school, he was forced to repeatedly borrow from his literary agent, a man named Harold Ober.

Desperate for cash, in 1937 Fitzgerald once again found work in Hollywood, where he took a role as part of a screenwriting staff for Metro-Goldwyn-Mayer. The gig paid well enough, with a steady paycheck of $1,000 a week. It was with this money that Fitzgerald was able to slowly but surely pay off the huge debts he had accrued. More importantly for his own personal health, he also managed to stop drinking. Although he was surrounded by younger staff writers who drank and caroused with the best of them, Fitzgerald began to choose Coca-Cola over hard liquor. He would drink vast quantities of soda, along with a heavy dose of candy consumption, as a substitute for his old habit of alcohol.

One bright spot of Fitzgerald's life during this period was a relationship he struck up with a woman named Sheilah Graham. Originally from Britain, Sheilah had made her way to Hollywood to work as a gossip columnist. Although Scott had had his own fair share of gossip hurled at him, he was immediately smitten by this charming young woman. Unfortunately, Fitzgerald would unravel when he took a flight with Sheilah later that year to Chicago, accompanying her for a radio broadcast she was taking part in. He broke his sobriety mid-flight by imbibing large amounts of alcohol and wound up getting into an altercation with the producer of the radio show.

Picking himself up from this bad relapse, Fitzgerald made his way back to Hollywood, where in January of 1938, he began work on a screenplay for a movie titled *Infidelity*. Some of the more risqué elements of the script were frowned upon by the strict limitations of what Hollywood could produce in those days.

It was while the big wigs in Hollywood were considering what to do with Fitzgerald's draft of the script that the writer decided to take his wife and daughter on an outing to Virginia Beach. This may have been an attempt to patch up his floundering marriage, but he certainly didn't make much progress. Faced with his wife's continued mental decline, Scott once again hit the booze, and the vacation turned into a nonstop session of arguing and alcohol-fueled incoherence.

When Fitzgerald returned to Hollywood, a concerned Sheilah had him sent off to a clinic to recover. She realized now more than anyone else that alcohol was slowly killing her friend, so in order to take him away from the temptation of alcohol so common among his peers, she convinced him to rent a home in Malibu, which would separate him from the other writers.

Fitzgerald only remained at his Malibu home for a brief time, and by the fall of 1938, he had moved on to San Fernando Valley, where he was able to rent a place on the cheap. Being able to save money like this proved a necessity since, by the end of the year, MGM decided to drop him completely. Shortly thereafter, Fitzgerald appeared to get a big break in the form of being enlisted to create a movie adaptation of the wildly popular novel *Gone with the Wind*. Like many times before, however, things did not work out, and Fitzgerald was terminated from the job just a couple of weeks later.

This cycle of disaster seemed only to continue when Fitzgerald was brought onto a project with United Artists to work on a script for a film called *Winter Carnival* based on a girl who goes back to a winter carnival at her old college and falls in love. This gig had him working with a much younger writer by the name of Budd Schulberg.

In February of 1939, Scott and Budd visited the carnival at Dartmouth College, which was the backdrop of the film. This proved a mistake since reliving college life quite predictably prompted Fitzgerald to relive his drinking. He went on a bad boozing spree and began to get out of hand. Although his antics might have been somewhat cute in his early twenties, now that he was in his early forties, it was all terribly embarrassing. Not only that, but his antics managed to get both him and Budd Schulberg fired.

Upon his return to California, Sheilah once again swooped to the rescue and had Fitzgerald checked into a clinic so that he could sober up. The episode essentially had him blacklisted from

Hollywood. Now even the possibility of writing screenplays had been removed from his ever-shrinking list of literary opportunities. Fitzgerald now had no choice but to turn back to writing short stories. Several of these stories starred a fictionalized character of himself named Pat Hobby, a troubled screenwriter who was constantly failing to make it in Hollywood.

During this period in April of 1939, Scott also had one last excursion with Zelda. He took her with him on vacation to Havana, Cuba. Once again, the trip was largely one of incoherent squabbling. After their return stateside, the two went their separate ways. Fitzgerald was yet again desperate and depressed, and his increasingly intolerable ill-humor managed to drive all of his remaining friends away. Even the hitherto loyal Sheilah was unable to handle his harangues and parted from Scott for a few weeks.

The only high point during this period was Fitzgerald being able to sell the rights to his story "Babylon Revisited." The story would later be revised and adapted into the film *The Last Time I Saw Paris*, starring none other than Elizabeth Taylor. It was the income from the selling of his copyrights to this tale that would help F. Scott

Fitzgerald survive another year. Little did he know that it would be the last year of his life.

In late 1940, Fitzgerald had been working feverishly to finish his next full-length novel, a piece called *The Last Tycoon*. He had attempted to get the novel published in serial form but had been turned down. Undaunted, he continued to write the book even though the prospects for marketing it had become exceedingly dim.

Fitzgerald's health was in serious decline by this point, and in November of 1940, he suffered his first heart attack. He was browsing around in a local drugstore when his alcohol-weakened heart simply gave out. Sheilah, who by now had patched up her relationship with Scott, came rushing to his side. Concerned for his well-being, she had him move into her apartment with her.

On December 20, 1940, Scott, after putting aside his work on *The Last Tycoon*, left to take in a movie with Sheilah. On the way back, he began to suffer from heart palpitations, and Sheilah rushed him home. Scott was planning to see the doctor the next day, but he wouldn't get the chance. The next morning, while reading the newspaper, he suddenly fell to the floor, unresponsive. Sheilah was right there with him and did her best to summon aid, but it was too late. F. Scott Fitzgerald was gone. He was only 44.

Conclusion

Scott Fitzgerald always dreamed of rising above his meager roots and attaining something great. The interesting thing about Fitzgerald is that he did indeed become successful—but his success came so soon, and so early in life, that he was largely ill-prepared for it. Almost like a butterfly coming out of its cocoon too soon, F. Scott Fitzgerald emerged on the scene ill-prepared for the high society life that he so desperately craved.

After the smash success of *This Side of Paradise*, Fitzgerald had money to burn and wild oats to sow. If perhaps his success had come a few years later, he would have been able to handle it a bit more maturely. But as it were, he bloomed early as a professional writer but then found himself unable to recapture the magic he had achieved as a young man. The rest of his life was a giant catch-up game, in which he would try to recreate the massive success he experienced early on yet find himself altogether unable to do so.

It wasn't that his written material was bad—on the contrary, as the passage of time has proven, novels such as *The Great Gatsby* were brilliant and have since become true cult classics. It was just that Fitzgerald had found himself at odds with the very times that he lived in. He came to prominence on the high tides of the Roaring Twenties, but by the end of the decade, the world had moved on—even though he had not. As a result, Fitzgerald at the end of his life found himself pigeonholed in stylistic trappings that the post-Great Depression world just didn't care for. For the rest of the world, the thrill of the Roaring Twenties was over, and the hang-over of the Great Depression loomed too large to appreciate much else.

It would take quite a few more years for Fitzgerald's work to once again captivate new generations of readers. Nevertheless, many years after his death, F. Scott Fitzgerald has indeed proven himself to be one of the greatest writers of all time.

Bibliography

Brown, David S. (2017). *Paradise Lost: A Life of F. Scott Fitzgerald.*

Donaldson, Scott (1983). *Fool for Love: F. Scott Fitzgerald.*

Fitzgerald, F. Scott (2004). *Conversations with F. Scott Fitzgerald.*

Fitzgerald, Zelda (1991). *The Collected Writings of Zelda Fitzgerald.*

Graham, Sheilah; Frank, Gerold (1958). *Beloved Infidel: The Education of a Woman.*

Kruse, Horst H. (2014). *F. Scott Fitzgerald at Work: The Making of 'The Great Gatsby'.*

Territore, John (2001). *F. Scott Fitzgerald: The American Dreamer.*

Turnbull, Andrew (1954). *Scott Fitzgerald.*

Printed in Great Britain
by Amazon